TREASURED

JOSHUA G. ALEXANDER

God loves you so very much, exactly as you are right at this moment. You are one of a kind. No one has been, is or will ever be just like you, you are God's masterpiece - right now.

Ephesians 2:10 For we are His workmanship (His own master work, a work of art) created in Christ Jesus (reborn from above-- spiritually transformed, renewed, ready to be used) for good works, which God prepared (for us) beforehand (taking paths which He set), so that we would walk in them (living the good life which He prearranged and made ready for us).

Ephesians 1:4-5 Just as (in His love) He chose us in Christ (actually selected us for Himself as His own) before the foundation of the world, so that we would be holy (that is, consecrated, set apart for Him, purpose-driven) and blameless in His sight. In love. He predestined and lovingly planned for us to be adopted to Himself as (His own) children through Christ Jesus, in accordance with the kind intention and good pleasure of His will --

God's love does not start or stop whether you do kind or cruel things, it does not stop or start if you talk hurtfully about others or their choices. God's love begins the second we exist inside our mommies and it never stops…never.

Psalm 39:13-16. For You formed my innermost parts; You knit me together in my mother's womb. I will give thanks and praise to You, for I am fearfully and wonderfully made; wonderful are Your works, and my soul knows it very well. My frame was not hidden from You, when I was being formed in secret, and intricately and skillfully formed (as if embroidered with many colors) in depths of the earth. Your eyes have seen my unformed substance; and in Your book were all written the days that were appointed for me, when as yet there was not one of them (even taking shape).

Isaiah 49:16 Indeed, I have inscribed (a picture of) you on the palms of My hands;...

Ephesians 2:8 For it is by grace (God's remarkable compassion and favor drawing you to Christ) that you have been saved (actually delivered from judgment and given eternal life) through faith. And this (salvation) is not of yourselves (not through your own effort), but it is the (undeserved, gracious) gift of God.

You cannot win God's love like in a game, you cannot earn God love like a sticker, award or trophy, you cannot stop God's love even if you don't want it or know about His love. God loves you because He wants to love you.

Isaiah 54:10 "For the mountains may be removed and the hills may shake, but My lovingkindness will not be removed from you, nor will My covenant of peace be shaken," says the Lord who has compassion on you.

Ephesians 1:5. He predestined and lovingly planned for us to be adopted to Himself as (His own) children through Jesus Christ, in accordance with the kind intention and good pleasure of His will—

Luke 23:34. And Jesus was saying, "Father, forgive them; for they do not know what they are doing." And they cast lots, dividing His clothes among themselves.

Luke 23:39-43 One of the criminals who had been hanged (on a cross beside Him) kept hurling abuse at Him, saying, "Are You not the Christ? Save Yourself and us (from death)! But the other one rebuked him, saying, "Do you not even fear God, since you are under the same sentence of condemnation? We are suffering justly, because we are getting what we deserve for what we have done; but this Man has done nothing wrong." And he was saying, "Jesus, (please) remember me when You come into Your kingdom!" Jesus said to him, "I assure you and most solemnly say to you, today you will be with Me in Paradise."

When good things happen, God loves you. When bad things happen, God loves you. God is always with you, God helps you to get through the bad things.

Psalm 56:8 You have taken account of my wanderings; put my tears in Your bottle. Are they not recorded in Your book?

Psalm 27:10 Although my father and my mother have abandoned me, yet the Lord will take me up (adopt me as His child).

Psalm 10:17-18 O Lord, you have heard the desire of the humble and oppressed; You will strengthen their heart, You will incline Your ear to hear, to vindicate and obtain justice for the fatherless and the oppressed.

If you trip and fall to the ground, it hurts, you know how it feels. After, if you see someone else trip and fall, you remember how it hurt, how it felt, you can better help them. Sometimes God helps us to use our hurts to better help others.

Isaiah 41:9-13. You whom I (the Lord) have taken from the ends of the earth, and called from its remotest parts, and said to you, 'You are My servant, I have chosen you and have not rejected you (even though you are exiled). Do not fear (anything), for I am with you; do not be afraid, for I am your God. I will strengthen you, be assured I will help you; I will certainly take hold of you with My righteous right hand (a hand of justice, of power, of victory, of salvation).' Indeed, all those who are angry with you will be put to shame and humiliated; those who strive against you will be as nothing and will perish. You shall search for those who quarrel with you, but will not find them; they who war against you will be as nothing, as nothing at all. For I the Lord your God keep hold of your right hand; (I am the Lord), who says to you, 'Do not fear, I will keep you.

Good and bad things happen to everyone. God might not explain why bad things happen —but, God did send His Son Jesus to make up for all the bad things that happen to us and for the bad things we might do too.

Romans 11:33-35 Oh, the depth of the riches and wisdom and knowledge of God! How unsearchable are His judgments and decisions and how unfathomable and untraceable are His ways! For who has known the mind of the Lord, or who has been His counselor? Or who has first given to Him that it would be paid back to him?

2 Peter 3:9 For the Lord does not delay (as though He were unable to act), and is not slow about HIS promise, as some count slowness, but is (extraordinarily) patient toward you, not wishing for any to perish but for all to come to repentance

To understand why bad things happen at all we would have to have a forever God-brain, but we only have a one-lifetime human- brain. That's why we cannot understand. Grown-ups use the word mystery to explain what we cannot understand, the word puzzle is good too.

Isaiah 55:8-9 For My thoughts are not your thoughts, nor are your ways My ways," declares the Lord. "For as the heavens are higher than the earth, so are My ways higher than your ways and My thoughts higher than your thoughts."

1 John 4:9-10 By this the love of God was displayed in us, in that God has sent His (One and) only begotten Son (the One who is truly unique, the only One of His kind) into the world so that we might live through Him. In this is love, not that we loved God, but that He loved us and sent His Son to be the propitiation (that is, the atoning sacrifice, and the satisfying offering) for our sins (fulfilling God's requirement for justice against sin and placating His wrath).

God wants to be your best friend. God wants to hear about your favorite toys, games, sports, animals, parks, trees, flowers,…. everything and anything. God wants to talk about what you want to talk about, or, if you just want to be quiet with God like when you are quiet with your best friend, God likes that too.

Psalm 147:3 He heals the brokenhearted

And binds up their wounds [healing their pain and comforting their sorrow].

Psalm 103:17-18 But the loving kindness of the Lord is from everlasting to everlasting on those who (reverently) fear Him, And His righteousness to children's children. To those who honor and keep His covenant, and remember to do His commandments (imprinting His word on their hearts).

Proverbs 3:5-6 Trust in and rely confidently on the Lord with all your heart. And do not rely on your own insight or understanding. In all your ways know and acknowledge and recognize Him, and He will make your paths straight and smooth (removing obstacles that block your way).

Thank God every day for being alive, for seeing, hearing, smelling, talking, touching, walking, jumping, running, playing — thank God for all good things and ask God to help you learn from the sad things.

John 3:17 For God did not send the Son into the world to judge and condemn the world (that is, to initiate the final judgment of the world), but that the world might be saved through Him.

John 5:24 I assure you and most solemnly say to you, the person who hears My word [the one who heeds My message], and believes and trusts in Him who sent Me, has (possesses now) eternal life [that is, eternal life actually begins—the believer is transformed], and does not come into judgment and condemnation, but has passed [over] from death into life.

Romans 8:1 Therefore there is now no condemnation [no guilty verdict, no punishment] for those who are in Christ Jesus [who believe in Him as personal Lord and Savior].

Ask God for help anytime and God will answer. Remember, God might not answer when we think it is best to answer, but God will answer when He knows that it is best to answer because He cares so much . Remember God is using His forever God- brain to answer us, we use our human brain.

Psalm 37:4-5 Delight yourself in the Lord, and He will give you the desires and petitions of your heart. Commit your way to the Lord; trust in Him also and He will do it.

Jeremiah 29:11 'For I know the plans and thoughts that I have for you,' says the Lord, 'plans for peace and well-being and not for disaster, to give you a future and a hope.

1 Peter 5:6-7 Therefore humble yourselves under the mighty hand of God [set aside self-righteous pride], so that He may exalt you [to a place of honor in His service] at the appropriate time, casting all your cares [all your anxieties, all your worries, and all your concerns, once and for all] on Him, for He cares about you [with deepest affection, and watches over you very carefully].

God wants you to have the best life you possibly can right now because God loves you all the time…now and forever.

Psalm 47:11 The Lord favors those who fear and worship Him (with awe-inspired reverence and obedience), those who wait for His mercy and loving kindness.

Joshua 10:25 Joshua said to them, "Do not fear or be dismayed (intimidated)! Be strong and courageous, for this is what the Lord will do to all your enemies against whom you (are about to) fight.

John 10:9-11 I am the Door; anyone who enters through Me will be saved (and will live forever), and will go in and out (freely), and find pasture (spiritual security). The thief comes only in order to steal and kill and destroy, I came that they may have and enjoy life, and have it in abundance (to the full, till it overflows). I am the Good Shepherd. The Good Shepherd lays down His (own) life for the sheep.

WestBow Press books may be ordered through booksellers or by contacting:

WestBow Press
A Division of Thomas Nelson & Zondervan
1663 Liberty Drive
Bloomington, IN 47403
www.westbowpress.com
844-714-3454

All Scripture quotations are taken from the Amplified® Bible (AMPC), Copyright © 1954, 1958, 1962, 1964, 1965, 1987 by The Lockman Foundation. Used by permission.

ISBN: 978-1-6642-2414-8 (sc)
ISBN: 978-1-6642-2415-5 (e)

Library of Congress Control Number: 2021903330

Print information available on the last page.

WestBow Press rev. date: 03/10/2021

WESTBOW
PRESS®
A DIVISION OF THOMAS NELSON
& ZONDERVAN

Printed in the United States
by Baker & Taylor Publisher Services